===WORDSWORTH ART PRINTS===

The Portfolio Book

—of the—

IMPRESSIONISTS

© 1995 English language edition, Wordsworth Editions Limited
Cumberland House, Crib Street, Ware Hertfordshire SG 12 9ET

ISBN 1 85326 861 5

© 1995, Royal Smeets Offset b.v., Weert, The Netherlands

For works of visual artists affiliated with a CISAC-organization the copyrights have been
settled with Beeldrecht at Amsterdam, The Netherlands. © 1995 c/o Beeldrecht.

Production, VBI/Smeets.

Printed and bound by Royal Smeets Offset b.v., Weert, The Netherlands.

IMPRESSIONISM

The art movement known as Impressionism, which arrived on the scene in France in the mid-nineteenth century, is generally regarded as having pioneered modern art. Probably for the first time in art history, a distinct schism arose between what was accepted by the art establishment in the way of themes and styles and a new group of artists who chose their own subject matter and interpreted it according to their individual predilections.

On the one hand, there was the majority of painters who conformed to the unstated dictates of the official government exhibition, the Salon. On the other hand there emerged a series of artists who were vilified by the established art world, the public and the critics of their day for their revolutionary adventures and experimentation on canvas but who are now regarded as the great imaginative artists of the French school in the 19th century.

The painter who is generally regarded as the real father of the Impressionist school is Edouard Manet, who scandalised the public by his painting of the nude, by his use of pure flat colours almost without shadow and by his great simplification of composition.

The first signs of the controversy appeared at the Salon of 1863, when so many works were refused by the jury that the government permitted the disappointed painters to exhibit in the *Salon des Refusés*. Here Manet shocked the public with his *Déjeuner sur l'herbe*, a startling portrait of a nude woman and two clothed men seated in a glade.

Two years later his *Olympia* again brought protest from the public. The scandal provoked by these two paintings confused the issue as to the merits of Impressionist painting for years to come.

The public, accustomed to thinking of art as idealised scenes of classic mythology, religious events or stirring moments in history, was unprepared and unwilling to grant the claims of everyday existence. From the mid-1860s such men as Claude Monet, Edgar Degas, Camille Pissarro, Jean-Frederic Bazille, Auguste Renoir and Alfred Sisley followed Manet's lead in depicting scenes of contemporary life and landscapes of the world in which they lived. Their rejection of artistic idealization and of literary anecdote was accompanied by a radical change in technique which was the logical consequence of a new approach to perceiving stimuli from the outside world.

Their eight co-operative exhibitions, held between 1874 and 1886, usually shocked the public, but gradually perceptive critics and collectors came to understand the importance of the movement. By the early 1880s Monet, Degas and Renoir had a considerable following, and their works were appreciated even outside France. For Pissarro and Sisley the struggle was more difficult, recognition coming to the former only in the 1890s.

Since landscape painting offered the most favorable opportunities for the study of nature and the contemporary scene, the series of works executed as variations of a single subject observed under changing climatic and light conditions - such as Monet's portrayals of haystacks and the facade of Rouen cathedral - are the most typical of all Impressionist work.

Degas was less interested in the painting of inanimate nature, to which the Impressionists usually attached such importance, but he exploited the use of chance effects on composition.

The figure paintings of Renoir and Degas, and the works Manet executed during the last ten years of his life, are revelations of the beauty, interest and pleasures of modern life.

Just as the landscapists had avoided anecdote and moralising, so the figure painters were content to depict whatever activities of modern men and women interested them without regard for conventional interpretations. Renoir's portraits, his bathers, peasants and pleasureseekers, and Degas' café and boudoir scenes are the realization of those aspects of contemporary life.

Impressionism has won a secure place in the history of art. Moreover, the Impressionists can be considered as the precursors and instigators of what is known as modern art.

Gustave Caillebotte, 1848-1894C
Sailing-Boats at Argenteuil, c.1880
Oil on canvas, 65 x 55 cm
Paris, Musée d'Orsay

Mary Cassatt, 1844-1926
Woman Sewing, 1880/82
Oil on canvas, 92 x 63 cm
Paris, Musée d'Orsay

Paul Cézanne, 1839-1906
The Suicide's House, 1880/82
Oil on canvas, 55 x 66 cm
Paris, Musée d'Orsay

Paul Cézanne, 1839-1906
Marseilles Bay seen from L'Estaque, 1878/79
Oil on canvas, 59 x 73 cm
Paris, Musée d'Orsay

Edgar Degas, 1834-1917
Two Laundresses, c.1884
Oil on canvas, 76 x 81,5 cm
Paris, Musée d'Orsay

Edgar Degas, 1834-1917
Racehorses in Front of the Stands, c.1879
Oil on canvas, 46 x 61 cm
Paris, Musée d'Orsay

Edgar Degas, 1834-1917
The Dancing Class, 1874
Oil on canvas, 85 x 75 cm
Paris, Musée d'Orsay

Edgar Degas, 1834-1917
Dancers on the Stage, 1878
Pastel on paper, 60 x 44 cm
Paris, Musée d'Orsay

Edgar Degas, 1834-1917
Dancer Posing for a Photographer, c.1879
Oil on paper, 31 x 28 cm
Moscow, Pushkin State Museum of Fine Arts

Edgar Degas, 1834-1917
The Singer in Gloves, 1878
Pastel on canvas, 53 x 41 cm
Cambridge (Mass.) Fogg Art Museum

Édouard Manet, 1832-1883
Argenteuil, 1874
Oil on canvas, 147 x 113 cm
Musée des Beaux-Arts, Tournai

Édouard Manet, 1832-1883
The Blonde with the Bare Breasts, 1875/78
Oil on canvas, 62,5 x 52 cm
Paris, Musée d'Orsay

Édouard Manet, 1832-1883
On the Beach, 1873
Oil on canvas, 59,6 x 73,2 cm
Paris, Musée d'Orsay

Édouard Manet, 1832-1883
Luncheon on the Grass, 1863
Oil on canvas, 208 x 264,5 cm
Paris, Musée d'Orsay

Édouard Manet, 1832-1883
Singer at the Café-Concert, c.1879
Oil on canvas, 93 x 74 cm
Private Collection

Claude Monet, 1840-1926
The Roches Noires Hotel at Trouville, 1870
Oil on canvas, 80 x 55 cm
Paris, Musée d'Orsay

Claude Monet, 1840-1926
Women in the Garden, 1866/67
Oil on canvas, 255 x 205 cm
Paris, Musée d'Orsay

Claude Monet, 1840-1926
The Church at Vétheuil, 1879
Oil on canvas, 65 x 50 cm
Paris, Musée d'Orsay

Claude Monet, 1840-1926
The Balcony, 1868/69
Oil on canvas, 169 x 125 cm
Paris, Musée d'Orsay

Claude Monet, 1840-1926
Water-Lilies, Harmony in Blue and Violet,
Oil on canvas, 200 x 201 cm
Paris, Musée Marmottan

Claude Monet, 1840-1926
The Houses of Parliament, London, 1903
Oil on canvas, 81,3 x 92,5 cm
Washington D.C., National Gallery of Art
Chester Dale Collection

Claude Monet, 1840-1926
Wild Poppies, 1873
Oil on canvas, 50 x 65 cm
Paris, Museé d'Orsay

Claude Monet, 1840-1926
The Bridge at Argenteuil, 1874
Oil on canvas, 60 x 80 cm
Paris, Museé d'Orsay

Claude Monet, 1840-1926
The Magpie, 1869
Oil on canvas, 89 x 130 cm
Paris, Musée d'Orsay

Berthe Morisot, 1841-1895
The Cradle, 1872
Oil on canvas, 56 x 46 cm
Paris, Musée d'Orsay

Camille Pissarro, 1830-1903
Entrance to the Village of Voisins, 1872
Oil on canvas, 46 x 55 cm
Paris, Musée d'Orsay

Camille Pissarro, 1830-1903
Little Bridge at Pontoise, 1875
Oil on canvas, 65 x 81 cm
Mannheim, Städtische Kunsthalle

Pierre Auguste Renoir, 1841-1919
Girls by the Seashore, 1894
Oil on canvas, 55 x 46 cm
Private Collection

Pierre Auguste Renoir, 1841-1919
Portrait of Jeanne Samary, 1877
Oil on canvas, 56 x 45 cm
Moscow, Pushkin State Museum of Fine Arts

Pierre Auguste Renoir, 1841-1919
The Loge, 1874
Oil on canvas, 80 x 64 cm
London, The Courtauld Institute Galleries

Pierre Auguste Renoir, 1841-1919
Her First Evening out, c.1880
Oil on canvas, 65 x 50 cm
London, The Tate Gallery

Pierre Auguste Renoir, 1841-1919
Girls at the Piano, 1892
Oil on canvas, 116 x 90 cm
Paris, Musée d'Orsay

Pierre Auguste Renoir, 1841-1919
Bather, 1882
Oil on canvas, 54 x 39 cm
Private Collection

Alfred Sisley, 1839-1899
Snow at Louveciennes, 1878
Oil on canvas, 61 x 50 cm
Paris, Musée d'Orsay

Alfred Sisley, 1839-1899
Field-guard in the Forest of Fontainebleau, 1870
Oil on canvas, 78 x 63 cm
Private Collection

Henri de Toulouse-Lautrec, 1864-1901
The Englishwoman at the "Star",
Le Havre, 1899
Oil on panel, 41 x 32,8 cm
Albi, Musée de Toulouse-Lautrec

Henri de Toulouse-Lautrec, 1864-1901
La Passagère du 54, 1896
Lithograph, 59 x 39,7 cm

Henri de Toulouse-Lautrec, 1864-1901
A Passing Fancy, 1896
Oil on canvas, 103 x 65 cm
Toulouse, Musée des Augustins

Henri de Toulouse-Lautrec, 1864-1901
Jockey on his Way to the Scales, 1899
Lithograph, 40,2 x 29 cm

Henri de Toulouse-Lautrec, 1864-1901
Cha-U-Kao at the Moulin Rouge, 1895
Oil on canvas, 75 x 55 cm
Winterthur, Oskar Reinhart Collection

How to Use this Book

Thirty-nine of the forty prints in this book are easily removed. Open the book and press it onto a flat surface, and grip the desired print firmly with the other hand. Pull it diagonally from the binding and it will come away leaving a clean edge. It is now ready for framing. The first print in the book may be cut away with a scalpel or knife. Alternatively, you may wish to keep the book intact as a valuable reference source.

The prints are suitable for framing using ready-made framing kits, available from framing, print and poster shops. The simplest of these kits are the clip-style frames which consist of a backing board, a sheet of backing paper (usually white with a black verso), a perspex or glass front and clips to hold the frame together. You can buy wooden frames complete with cut-out mount. There is a very large range of styles and prices for ready-made frames.